CHRISTMAS FAVORITES

Solos and Band Arrangements
Correlated with Essential Elements Band Method

ARRANGED BY
MICHAEL SWEENEY

Welcome to Essential Elements Christmas Favorites! There are two versions of each holiday selection in this versatile book:
1. The SOLO version (with lyrics) appears on the left-hand page.
2. The FULL BAND arrangement appears on the right-hand page.
Use the optional accompaniment tape when playing solos for friends and family. Your director may also use the accompaniment tape in band rehearsals and concerts.

ISBN 978-0-7935-1766-4

7777 W. BLUEMOUND RD. P.O. BOX 13819 MILWAUKEE, WI 53213

JINGLE BELLS

AUXILIARY PERCUSSION
SLEIGH BELLS
Band Arrangement

Words and Music by J. PIERPONT
Arranged by MICHAEL SWEENEY

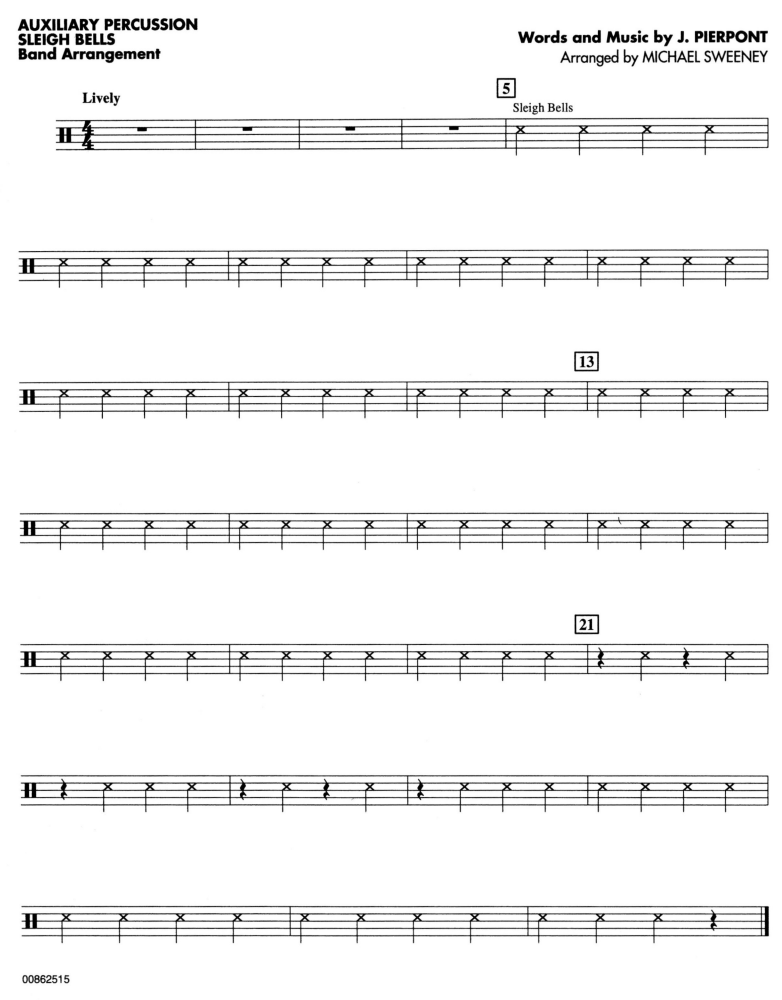

00862515

JINGLE BELLS

**PERCUSSION
SNARE DRUM, BASS DRUM
Band Arrangement**

Words and Music by J. PIERPONT
Arranged by MICHAEL SWEENEY

00862515

AUXILIARY PERCUSSION
TRIANGLE
Band Arrangement

Arranged by MICHAEL SWEENEY

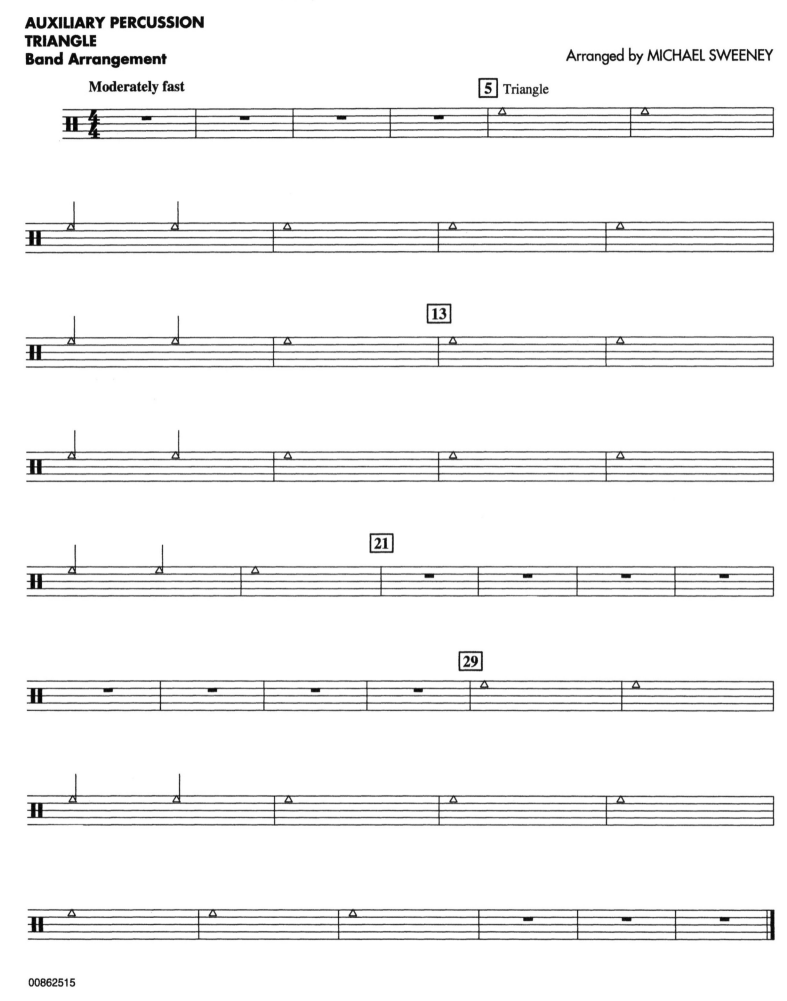

UP ON THE HOUSETOP

PERCUSSION
SNARE DRUM, BASS DRUM
Band Arrangement

Arranged by MICHAEL SWEENEY

00862515

AUXILIARY PERCUSSION
TAMBOURINE
Band Arrangement

Arranged by MICHAEL SWEENEY

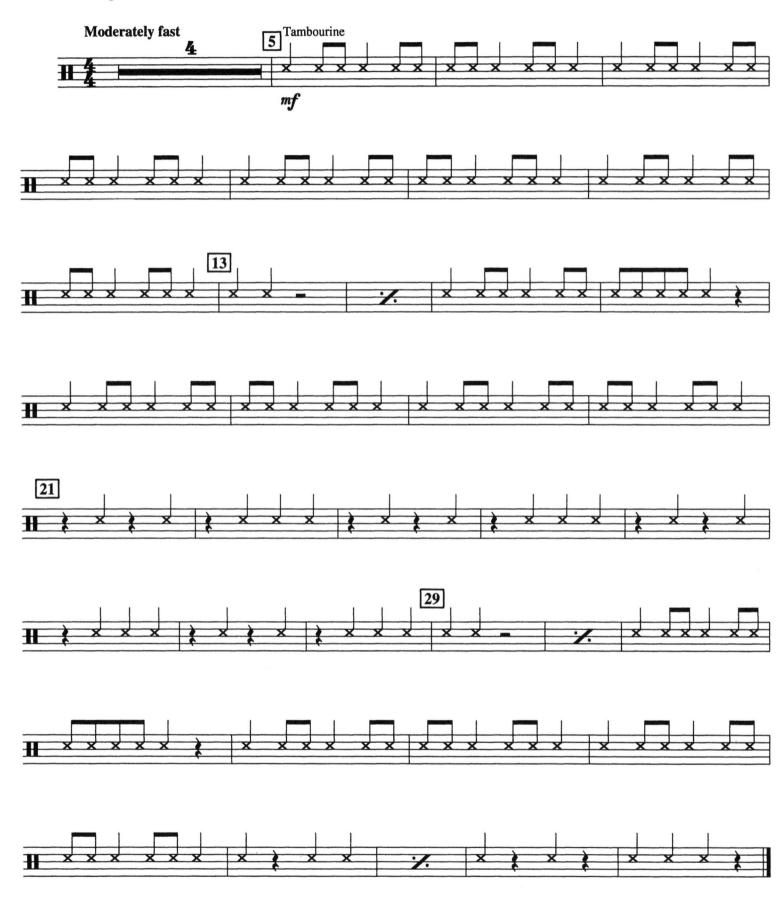

00862515

T E ANUKK S N

PERCUSSION
SNARE DRUM, BASS DRUM
Band Arrangement

Arranged by MICHAEL SWEENEY

00862515

AUXILIARY PERCUSSION
SUSPENDED CYMBAL, SHAKER
Band Arrangement

Music and Lyrics by JOHNNY MARKS
Arranged by MICHAEL SWEENEY

PERCUSSION
SNARE DRUM, BASS DRUM
Band Arrangement

Music and Lyrics by JOHNNY MARKS
Arranged by MICHAEL SWEENEY

*Rim Knocks: Hold middle of S.D. stick firmly with left hand. Place tip of stick on the head (center)
and keep it there while striking rim with butt end of stick.

00862515

AUXILIARY PERCUSSION
CR. CYM., TRI., SLEIGH BELLS
Band Arrangement

Arranged by MICHAEL SWEENEY

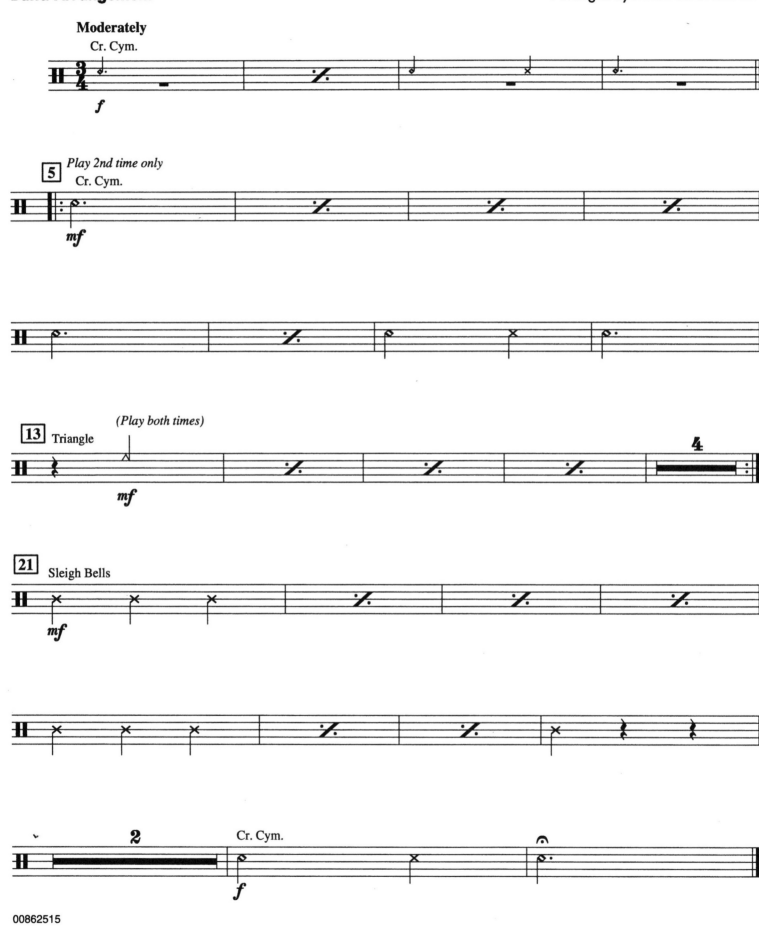

00862515

PERCUSSION
SNARE DRUM, BASS DRUM
Band Arrangement

Arranged by MICHAEL SWEENEY

00862515

FROSTY THE SNOWMAN

AUXILIARY PERCUSSION
SLEIGH BELLS, CRASH CYMBALS
Band Arrangement

Words and Music by STEVE NELSON and JACK ROLLINS
Arranged by MICHAEL SWEENEY

00862515

FROSTY THE SNOWMAN

PERCUSSION
SNARE DRUM, BASS DRUM
Band Arrangement

Words and Music by STEVE NELSON and JACK ROLLINS
Arranged by MICHAEL SWEENEY

ROCKIN' AROUND THE CHRISTMAS TREE

AUXILIARY PERCUSSION
CR. CYM., SLEIGH BELLS,
SUS. CYM., TAMB.
Band Arrangement

Music and Lyrics by JOHNNY MARKS
Arranged by MICHAEL SWEENEY

00862515

ROCKIN' AROUND THE
CHRISTMAS TREE

PERCUSSION
SNARE DRUM, BASS DRUM
Band Arrangement

Music and Lyrics by JOHNNY MARKS
Arranged by MICHAEL SWEENEY

JINGLE-BELL ROCK

AUXILIARY PERCUSSION
SUS. CYM., SLEIGH BELLS
Band Arrangement

Words and Music by JOE BEAL
and JIM BOOTHE
Arranged by MICHAEL SWEENEY

JINGLE-BELL ROCK

Words and Music by JOE BEAL
and JIM BOOTHE
Arranged by MICHAEL SWEENEY

PERCUSSION
SNARE DRUM, BASS DRUM
Band Arrangement

AUXILIARY PERCUSSION
CR. CYM., TRI., SUS. CYM., SHAKER
Band Arrangement

Music and Lyrics by JOHNNY MARKS
Arranged by MICHAEL SWEENEY

Moderately slow
Cr. Cym.

Play
Triangle

2

Moderate Bossa
Sus. Cym. with S.D. Stick

11

Shaker

mf

19

f

on dome of cym.

27

mf

2

35

f

1.

2.

RUDOLPH THE RED-NOSED REINDEER

PERCUSSION
SNARE DRUM, BASS DRUM
Band Arrangement

Music and Lyrics by JOHNNY MARKS
Arranged by MICHAEL SWEENEY

LET IT SNOW! LET IT SNOW! LET IT SNOW!

AUXILIARY PERCUSSION
SUS. CYM., SLEIGH BELLS
Band Arrangement

Words by SAMMY CAHN
Music by JULE STYNE
Arranged by MICHAEL SWEENEY

Lively

Sus. Cym. with S.D. stick

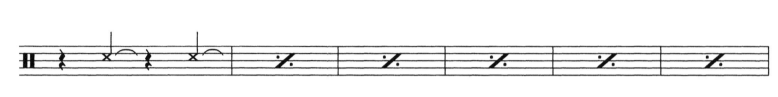

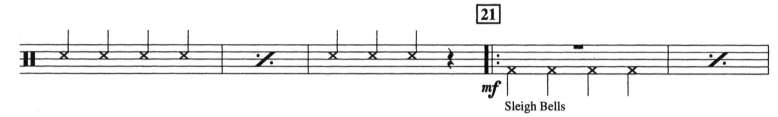

Sleigh Bells

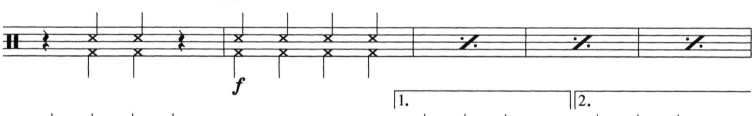

00862515

LET IT SNOW! LET IT SNOW! LET IT SNOW!

Words by SAMMY CAHN
Music by JULE STYNE
Arranged by MICHAEL SWEENEY

PERCUSSION
SNARE DRUM, BASS DRUM
Band Arrangement

00862515

T E H I TM   N

Music and Lyric by MEL TORME and ROBERT WELLS
Arranged by MICHAEL SWEENEY

AUXILIARY PERCUSSION
2 SUSPENDED CYMBALS, SLEIGH BELLS
Band Arrangement

THE CHRISTMAS SONG

PERCUSSION
SNARE DRUM, BASS DRUM
Band Arrangement

Music and Lyric by MEL TORME and ROBERT WELLS
Arranged by MICHAEL SWEENEY

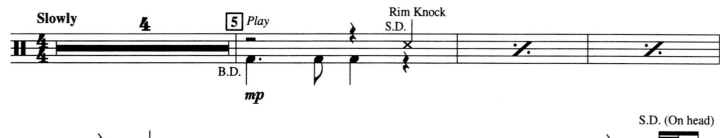

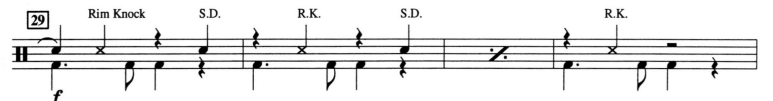

00862515